The Ultimate *Kangaroo* Book for Kids

100+ Amazing Kangaroo Facts, Photos, Quiz + More

Jenny Kellett

BELLANOVA

MELBOURNE · SOFIA · BERLIN

Copyright © 2026 by Jenny Kellett
The Ultimate Kangaroo Book for Kids
www.bellanovabooks.com

Image on pg. 22 copyright JJ Harrison (https://www.jjharrison.com.au/)
Image on pg. 20 copyright Donald Hobern from Copenhagen, Denmark
Image on page 30 copyright Flagstaff Photos

All rights reserved. No part of this book may be reproduced in any form by any electronic or mechanical means including photocopying, recording, or information storage and retrieval without permission in writing from the author.

Imprint: Bellanova Books
ISBN: 978-619-7695-97-7

Contents

Introduction 4
Kangaroos: The Basics 6
   Red Kangaroo 16
   Antilopine Kangaroo 20
   Western Grey Kangaroo 24
   Eastern Grey Kangaroo 28
Kangaroo Lifestyle 32
Breeding and Babies 51
Wallabies 62
Tree Kangaroos 64
Kangaroos and Us 66
Kangaroo Quiz 72
   Quiz Answers 77
Word Search Puzzle 78
Sources 81

Introduction

It's hard not to fall in love with the adorable kangaroo. Like much of Australia's wildlife, kangaroos are unique. Their joeys live in pouches, they hop to get around and they can freeze their embryos. Crazy, right?

We're going to learn more about these facts and much more. And don't forget to test yourself in our kangaroo quiz at the end.

Are you ready? *Let's go*!

Let's hop in.

What are kangaroos and where do they live?

Kangaroos belong to the marsupial group of animals, which are part of the macropod family.

• • •

Macropod means 'big foot'.

• • •

You can recognise a marsupial because it carries its young in a pouch. Other marsupials include koalas, wombats, and the Tasmanian devil.

Eastern Grey Kangaroos.

A red kangaroo flexing his muscles.

The kangaroo is the largest of the marsupials.

• • •

Kangaroos are **mammals**, meaning they give birth to live young — although, in a much different way than other mammals.

• • •

Kangaroos are indigenous to Australia and New Guinea, meaning that they can't be found in the wild anywhere else in the world.

It's hard to get an exact number, but it's estimated that over 34 million kangaroos live in Australia — that's higher than the human population!

• • •

Kangaroos live in groups called **mobs**.

• • •

There are typically around ten females, one or two males in a mob, plus the joeys.

• • •

The members of a mob are very caring towards each other. They will groom each other and protect one another from danger.

Eastern grey kangaroo.

Kangaroos are very social creatures, so they're rarely found on their own.

• • •

Kangaroos don't like to go too far from home. Their home territory is quite small, but they will travel further if there isn't enough food.

• • •

There are four main species of kangaroos: the **red kangaroo, the Antilopine kangaroo, the eastern grey** and **the western grey**. Let's take a closer look at them!

RED KANGAROO

Scientific name: *Osphranter rufus*

The red kangaroo — sometimes called the red giant kangaroo — is the largest kangaroo species and the largest marsupial in the world.

They are very powerful and muscular and you can often see them boxing each other. It is best not to approach them in the wild as they have been known to try and box humans, too!

Red kangaroos can be quite large. For example, males can reach a height of 2 metres (6ft 7in) and weigh 90 kg (200 lb).

Distribution of the Red Kangaroo.
Source: Natural Earth and Myself

They mostly live in the hot desert and arid regions of Central Australia. They enjoy eating shrubs and occasionally insects.

Males have reddish-brown coats, while females have blue-grey fur. They have large pointy ears and square-shaped noses.

Female red kangaroos are lighter and faster than males. Because of this, and their blue-coloured fur, they are often called 'blue fliers'.

A unique trait of the red kangaroo is that the females have been known to adopt another female's joeys.

Red kangaroos usually live in smaller groups than other kangaroos. Between 2-4 members in a mob are normal.

ANTILOPINE KANGAROO

Scientific name: *Osphranter rufus*

Antilopine kangaroos live in the hills of tropical northern Australia.

They are slightly smaller, less muscular than red kangaroos, and incredibly fast.

It is easy to tell the male and female antilopine kangaroos apart.

Males have reddish-coloured coats, while the females are brown and grey. Also, male antilopine kangaroos are much larger than females.

Distribution of the Antilopine Kangaroo.
Source: Natural Earth and Myself

Antilopine kangaroos are grazers, meaning that they spend a lot of their time eating. Like all kangaroos, they are herbivores.

As they live in a very hot climate, you can often find groups of them gathering around a waterhole to stay cool and hydrated.

They have several sounds to communicate with eachother. A hiss is used as an alarm, while a mother may speak to her joeys with a soft cluck.

Antilopine kangaroos can give birth at any time of the year, but they prefer to do it before the wet season starts.

There is no shortage of antilopine kangaroos in the wild! They are not listed as threatened by the IUCN and are pretty easy to spot if you are in their area.

WESTERN GREY KANGAROO

Scientific name: *Macropus fuliginosus*

Western grey kangaroos are mostly found in southern Australia and on Kangaroo Island.

They live in all sorts of habitats, including wooded, coastal, and even urban areas. The south of Australia is much milder than the tropical north where the antilopine kangaroos live.

It is quite normal to see kangaroos around the cities of Adelaide and Perth, for example.

Distribution of the Western Grey Kangaroo.
Source: Natural Earth and Myself

Western grey kangaroos have brown coats and paler-coloured chests. They are smaller than red kangaroos.

Male western grey kangaroos can be up to twice the size of females.

It can be quite hard to tell the difference between a western and eastern grey kangaroo. However, western grey kangaroos are usually slightly darker and sometimes have a blackish patch around their elbows.

Although Aboriginal Australians have lived with western grey kangaroos for thousands of years, Europeans only discovered them in 1802 when explorer Matthew Flinders landed on Kangaroo Island, south of Adelaide.

EASTERN GREY KANGAROO

Scientific name: *Macropus giganteus*

Eastern grey kangaroos are sometimes called the forester kangaroo or the great grey kangaroo.

The eastern grey kangaroo is the most commonly spotted, as they live along the entire eastern coastline of Australia, where most of the human population lives.

They are the only kangaroo species that live in the island state of Tasmania.

Distribution of the Eastern Grey Kangaroo.
Source: Natural Earth and Myself

They look very similar to western grey kangaroos, except they have paler faces and a black tip on the end of their tails.

Although not as large as red kangaroos, they can still weigh up to 66kg (146lb) and stand almost 2m (6ft 7in) high.

Female eastern grey kangaroos are usually much smaller than males.

Unlike red kangaroos, eastern grey kangaroos love living in areas where there is a lot of rainfall.

They prefer to live in areas with lots of trees, but can also be found in grassy areas.

There are two subspecies of eastern grey species, one of which can only be found on the island-state of Tasmania.

Feeling hoppy!

Let's look at kangaroo biology, lifestyle, and food.

Kangaroos have powerful hind legs and short arms. Their back legs are what help them jump so high.

• • •

The second and third claws on their hind legs are joined together, which creates a unique cleaning claw. Koalas also have this.

Their front paws are very dexterous, meaning they can use them for grabbing and holding things, including food.

• • •

Kangaroos are the only large animals in the world that use hopping as a way of getting around.

• • •

An average red kangaroo hops at a speed of 20–25 km/h (12–16 mph). But they can go double that speed over short distances if necessary.

• • •

Kangaroos can jump up to 7 metres (23 feet) forward!

Although it varies between species, kangaroos live until around the age of 6 in the wild. In captivity, they may live to be over 20 years old.

• • •

Kangaroos don't have many natural predators.

• • •

Animals that have been introduced into Australia, such as foxes and feral cats and dogs, are a problem for kangaroos. But they can put up a good fight if attacked!

Like humans, cats, and many other animals, Kangaroos have single-chambered stomachs.

• • •

Kangaroos will sometimes regurgitate their food and chew it again before finally digesting it.

• • •

Kangaroos are very strict herbivores, meaning that they only eat plants.

• • •

Although all kangaroos are herbivores, different species have different diets.

Eastern grey kangaroos eat primarily grasses, while red kangaroos eat more shrubs. Smaller kangaroos will also eat mushrooms.

• • •

Because of the hot climate in much of Australia, you'll usually find kangaroos spending their days sleeping in the shades of trees. They come out early in the evenings to eat and hop around.

• • •

Animals that come out during twilight hours are called **crepuscular**.

Especially in the Outback, kangaroos don't have much access to water. So instead, they get most of their water from the succulents that they eat.

• • •

Kangaroos have very special teeth — much different to most other mammals. Their incisors can chew off grass very low to the ground, while their molars chew and grind their food.

• • •

Kangaroos can't walk backward. This is because their tails are too heavy.

The national emblem of Australia includes an emu and a kangaroo, both animals that can't walk backward. This symbolises that the country only moves forward.

• • •

Kangaroos don't fart or burp! When most mammals fart and burp, they release methane, but kangaroos instead convert most of the hydrogen from their fermented food into extra energy.

• • •

Kangaroos are good swimmers. If threatened, they will run into waterways to escape and use their powerful limbs to drown their attacker.

It is quite normal for kangaroos to fight. They will box each other and even balance on their tails to completely lift their bodies into the air to kick their opponent with their back legs.

• • •

It is primarily male kangaroos that fight. They will fight over a drinking spot or a female that they are trying to impress.

• • •

Most kangaroos are left-handed.

Male kangaroos are known as bucks, boomers, jacks, or old men, while females can be called does, flyers, or jills.

. . .

Kangaroo tails are incredibly powerful. They often use their tails as a fifth leg and can use it to propel themselves high into the air. They also use their tails for balance.

. . .

Why do kangaroos hop? Because they have to! They can't move their hind legs independently from one another.

Kangaroos don't have sweat glands. So, if they need to cool down they will lick themselves until they are soaking wet.

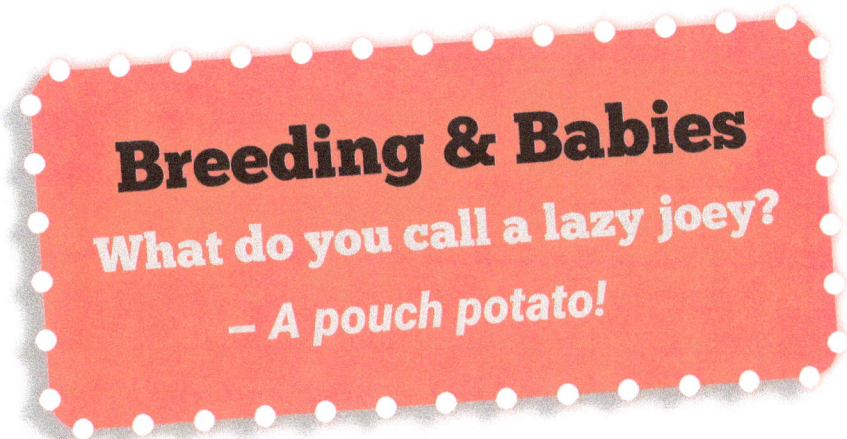

A young kangaroo is called a joey.

• • •

Kangaroos are only pregnant for about five weeks (33 days).

• • •

The scientific name for a kangaroo's pouch is the *marsupium*.

When a joey is born, it is around the size of a grape. It uses its tiny forearms to pull itself into its mother's pouch, where it will live for a few more months until it is fully formed.

• • •

Once the tiny joey has pulled itself into its mother's pouch for the first time, it takes one of its mother's teats, which expands inside its mouth. For the first few weeks, the milk automatically feeds the joey, but once it's more developed it can suckle on its own.

• • •

A female kangaroo has four teats.

Although kangaroos usually only give birth to one joey at a time, they can get pregnant while they still have a joey growing in their pouch.

Amazingly, when this happens, the mother can 'freeze' the younger joey until the older joey develops and leaves the pouch, at which point the female kangaroo sends hormone signals to restart the younger joey's growth.

...

Female kangaroos are almost always pregnant — which is one of the reasons why there are so many of them!

A female kangaroo can create different types of milk! If she has multiple joeys at different ages, she can change the nutritional content of the milk she feeds each of them.

...

Joeys will use their mother's pouches until they are about ten months old. They will butt their heads against the pouch if they want to get in for some milk.

...

Joeys not only feed in their pouch but they pee and poop in there too! So their mothers have to clean out the pouch regularly.

THE ULTIMATE KANGAROO BOOK

Although kangaroos don't have many predators, they have been known to drop their joeys out of their pouch and keep going if they are being attacked.

• • •

Male kangaroos can flex their muscles, just like humans do. They do this to impress females and scare off predators.

• • •

Female kangaroos can start breeding after 14 months, but usually have their first joey at around two years old.

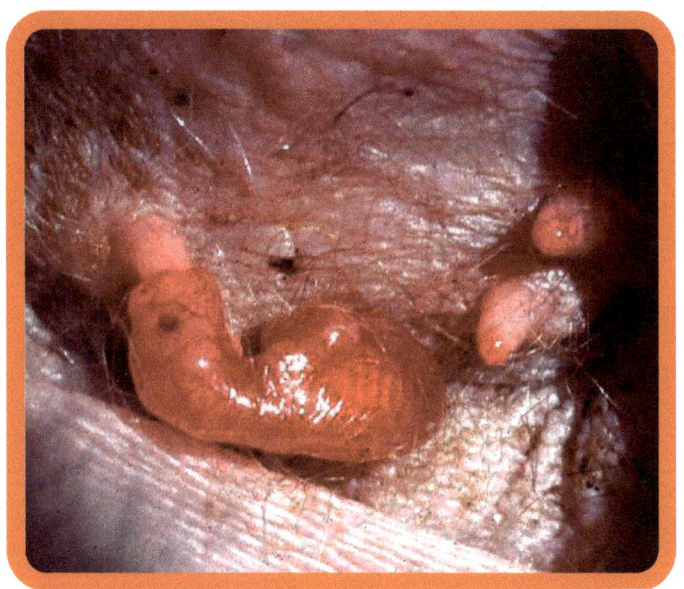

A newborn joey in its mother's pouch.
Image: Geoff Shaw @ http://kangaroo.genome.org.au

Kangaroos give birth sitting upright and hunched over. She will lick the fur inside her pouch to help make a pathway for the young joey to get out.

. . .

When joeys are born they are completely hairless and blind.

. . .

Joeys may accompany their mothers on short walks when they are six months old. By eight months old they will spend most of their time outside the pouch, although they may go back for warmth and milk — or a free ride!

Wallaby darned!

There is often a lot of confusion between kangaroos, wallabies and tree kangaroos. So let's take a closer look at the differences.

Wallabies

Wallabies look like kangaroos, and in many ways, they are very similar.

Wallabies are still macropods, but they are smaller than the kangaroos we have talked about.

There is also a middle-sized macropod called the **wallaroo**.

Wallabies are rarely above 20 kg, and half the height of a red kangaroo.

Wallabies also often have two or three different colours in their coats — some species are really quite colourful.

If you manage to look inside its mouth, you'll see that wallabies have flat teeth, while kangaroos have rounded teeth.

Tree Kangaroos

The tree kangaroo is another macropod, but it looks much different from the wallaby or kangaroo.

They are a dark red colour and live in the trees — the only macropod to do so.
Tree kangaroos also have larger tails, which help them to balance when moving through the trees.

Tree kangaroos live in the tropical rainforests of New Guinea and northeastern Australia. They are a threatened species, meaning that their numbers are declining. They are quite slow and clumsy, and

although they hop like other kangaroos, they do so much more slowly and awkwardly.

There are 12 different species of tree kangaroo, which live in various areas of New Guinea and Australia.

Watch out: Humans!
Kangaroos and Us

Although kangaroos are protected, it is quite normal to see a kangaroo burger on the menu in Australia. The meat is very healthy and high in protein.

• • •

Kangaroos are very important to Aboriginal Australians — both now and historically. For example, they provide meat, and their scrotums have been used to create balls for the traditional football game of *marngrook*.

Kangaroos are shy and don't pose much of a threat to humans. However, they will attack if they feel threatened. Red kangaroos are the most dangerous.

. . .

There has only been one official case of a human death caused by a kangaroo. This was in 1936.

. . .

A 2020 study found that kangaroos can communicate with humans by gazing and pointing with their eyes at what they want, similar to a dog.

In 2004 an eastern grey kangaroo received the RSPCA's *National Animal Valour Award* after alerting a family to an injured farmer.

• • •

The Australian one-dollar coin features five kangaroos.

• • •

Many sports teams in Australia have kangaroos as part of their name or emblem, such as Australia's national rugby league team (the Kangaroos) and Australia's national rugby team (the Wallabies).

Have you heard of *Skippy the Bush Kangaroo*? Many kids around the world loved watching this popular cartoon during the 1960s.

• • •

Sadly, 9 out of 10 animals killed on Australian roads are kangaroos. This is because kangaroos are attracted to the roads' shine and often sit there during the twilight hours. That is why it is crucial to be careful when driving at these times.

• • •

Australians living in rural areas must check the pouches of any female kangaroos that they find injured.

Kangaroo *Quiz*

Now test your knowledge in our Kangaroo Quiz!

1 What are the four main species of kangaroo?

2 What do you call a group of kangaroos?

3 Australia's national emblem features a kangaroo, and which other animal?

4 Which species of kangaroo is the largest?

5 Where do western grey kangaroos live?

6 Kangaroos are carnivores. True or false?

7 What group of animals does the kangaroo belong to?

8 In which two countries can you find wild kangaroos?

9 How long are kangaroos pregnant?

10 Kangaroos can walk backward. True or false?

11 How can you tell the difference between an eastern and western grey kangaroo?

12 Which Australian coin has five kangaroos on it?

13 Kangaroos are crepuscular. What does this mean?

14 What is a wallaroo?

15 How many species of tree kangaroo are there?

16 Kangaroos like to spend time alone. True or false?

17 When do kangaroos swim?

18 How many teats does a female kangaroo have?

19 How high can kangaroos jump?

20 Are kangaroos usually left-handed or right-handed?

Answers:

1. Red kangaroo, antilopine kangaroo, eastern grey and western grey kangaroo.
2. A mob.
3. An emu.
4. Red kangaroo.
5. In southern Australia.
6. False
7. Marsupials.
8. Australia and New Guinea.
9. Around 5 weeks (33 days).
10. False
11. Eastern grey kangaroos have paler faces and a black tip on the end of their tails.
12. One dollar coin.
13. They are most active during twilight hours.
14. A medium-sized marsupial, in between a kangaroo and a wallaby.
15. 12.
16. False
17. When they are in danger.
18. Four.
19. Seven metres (23 feet).
20. Left handed.

Kangaroo
WORD SEARCH

```
Q D A N T I L O P I N E
M V T U Z X C R D F Q D
A F R R S Q R M J H F S
R D E E F T D S O C X Z
S S W W O I R C S B X E
U V Z K A N G A R O O Z
P N V C X W A L L A B Y
I J B V D A H R F I A S
A B O S D F Q S Z D A V
L G C E H O P P I N G D
Z X C V Y B G F D S A C
O U T B A C K M N B V C
```

Can you find all the words below in the wordsearch puzzle on the left?

KANGAROO   WALLABY   HOPPING

JOEY   MOB   MARSUPIAL

AUSTRALIA   OUTBACK   ANTILOPINE

THE ULTIMATE KANGAROO BOOK

Solution

		A	N	T	I	L	O	P	I	N	E
M		U									
A				S			M				
R				T			O				
S					R			B			
U		K	A	N	G	A	R	O	O		
P			W	A	L	L	A	B	Y		
I	J							I			
A	O							A			
L		E	H	O	P	P	I	N	G		
		Y									
O	U	T	B	A	C	K					

Sources

"Kangaroo". 2014. Kids. https://kids.nationalgeographic.com/animals/mammals/kangaroo

"10 Incredible Facts About Kangaroos". 2021. Treehugger. https://www.treehugger.com/kangaroo-facts-5081686.

"Kangaroos use tail like a leg to walk". Australian Geographic. 2 July 2014. Retrieved 18 November 2014.

"15 Fun Facts About Kangaroos | The Fact Site". 2020. The Fact Site. https://www.thefactsite.com/kangaroo-facts/.

"Kangaroo". Parks Victoria. Archived from the original on 8 February 2011. Retrieved 2 February 2021.

Duran, Paulina. 2021. "Kangaroos Can Learn To Communicate With Humans, Researchers Say". U.S.. https://www.reuters.com/article/us-australia-wildlife-kangaroo-idUSKBN28Q0I9.

"Kangaroos: Facts, Information & Pictures | Live Science". 2021. Livescience.Com. https://www.livescience.com/27400-kangaroos.html.

"Red Kangaroo" National Geographic. https://www.nationalgeographic.com/animals/mammals/r/red-kangaroo/ . Accessed 4 Feb 2021.

"Eastern Gray Kangaroo | National Geographic". 2010. Animals. https://www.nationalgeographic.com/animals/mammals/e/eastern-gray-kangaroo/.

Riedman, Marianne L. (1982). "The Evolution of Alloparental Care in Mammals and Birds". The Quarterly Review of Biology. 57 (4): 405–435. doi:10.1086/412936. JSTOR 2826887.

"Eastern Grey Kangaroo". 2021. En.Wikipedia.Org. https://en.wikipedia.org/wiki/Eastern_grey_kangaroo.

"Macropod Reproduction (Kangaroo And Wallaby) | About The Roos | Kangaroo Creek Farm". 2021. Kangaroocreekfarm.Com. https://kangaroocreekfarm.com/about-roos/

"Libguides: Western Gray Kangaroo (Macropus Fuliginosus) Fact Sheet: Reproduction & Development". 2021. Ielc.Libguides.Com. https://ielc.libguides.com/sdzg/factsheets/westerngraykangaroo/reproduction.

"What Is The Difference Between A Kangaroo And A Wallaby?". 2021. Kangaroo Island Tours. https://kangarooislandtoursaustralia.com.au/blog/what-is-the-difference-between-a-kangaroo-and-a-wallaby

We hope you learned some awesome facts about kangaroos!

What was your favourite?

We'd love it if you took a moment to leave us a [review](#)—they always make us smile :) But more importantly, reviews help other readers make better decisions.

Thank you for your support!

Join us at www.bellanovabooks.com for the latest animal book releases and prize giveaways!

ALSO BY JENNY KELLETT

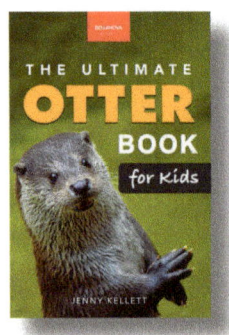

... and more!

Available at

www.bellanovabooks.com

and all major online bookstores.

www.ingramcontent.com/pod-product-compliance
Lightning Source LLC
LaVergne TN
LVHW050136080526
838202LV00061B/6494